Colen –
Merry Christmas
2015
Dick Kinney

"...I am here with good news for you, which will bring great joy to all people."

Luke 2:10

# The Nativity Dog

BY
RICHARD J. KINNEY

ART BY
SANDY HUSTON

xulon PRESS

## ACKNOWLEDGMENTS

A special thanks to my family, Suzie and the Kinney boys for their encouragement, guidance and proof reading skills.

Appreciation also goes to Andrea Drake for her spirit and friendly persuasion to complete this book, as well as to Mary Dougherty for her up-beat advice.

It was a joy to work with Sandy Huston whose art and creativity brought <u>The Nativity Dog</u> to life and with Nichole Nappi whose graphic design proved to be invaluable.

This story has never been told before.

It is about a dog named Calie and
the very first Christmas – the night
Jesus was born.

It all began in the town of Bethlehem.

At the time, many of the men worked as shepherds taking care of large flocks of sheep.

Some shepherds were fortunate to have their very own dog to help keep track of the sheep that grazed in open fields or on nearby rolling hills, where there were small caves.

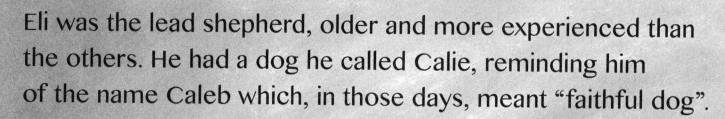

Eli was the lead shepherd, older and more experienced than the others. He had a dog he called Calie, reminding him of the name Caleb which, in those days, meant "faithful dog".

Calie was the best, smartest and bravest dog in all of Bethlehem.

Eli and Calie worked together tending their sheep in pastures near town. At the end of each day they herded their flock into a protected area near the hillside caves.

Each evening, at the front of the cave where he and Calie could still watch over the sheep, Eli would build a fire.

One very cold night he built an especially large and warm fire. The sky was crystal clear. The stars were brighter and more beautiful than ever before.

Just as Eli was about to fall asleep, Calie sat up.

The dog perked up his ears and looked around. He sensed that something special was happening and it was nearby.

Standing tall and alert at the edge of the cave,
Calie saw a bright light coming from Bethlehem
and he could hear singing.

What was going on?

While Calie was loyal to Eli, curiosity got the better of him and he scampered down the hill toward the light.

As he cautiously approached Bethlehem, the singing became clearer. The light now appeared as a dazzling star shining over a stable.

Calie became excited and ran toward the stable.
There was a bright light coming from inside
and he saw the outline of two people.

One person was kneeling on one knee and the other
was standing. They were both staring into a manger which
was often used to hold straw to feed animals.

As the dog got closer he saw there was
also a donkey, a cow and sheep in the stable.

Calie approached the front of the stable. He stretched out his paws in front of him. He put his head down and raised his eyes toward the manger. He wanted to go inside but he did not know if he was welcome.

Mary and Joseph were inside the stable.
Their new born baby, Jesus, was sleeping on
a bed of straw inside the manger.

Angels sang songs of joy as they hovered above.

The star over the stable was so brilliant it
seemed like daylight.

Mary saw the dog. She motioned to Joseph that they had a visitor. Joseph bent down and called for Calie to come into the stable.

The dog stood and walked over to him. Joseph petted him and rubbed him behind his ears.

Calie then circled around the manger and sat quietly beside Mary until, all of a sudden, he sprang to his feet when he heard movement in the straw.

Mary pointed toward the manger and invited Calie to look inside.

There he saw a baby wrapped in a white blanket surrounded by a glow of heavenly light.
For what seemed like a long time, the dog simply gazed at the baby. Then, unexpectedly, he backed away.

To Mary and Joseph's surprise, Calie turned abruptly and ran away. He had to get Eli.

The dog ran as fast as he could, up the hill to the cave where Eli was sleeping.

He nudged the shepherd with his nose until he was awake.

Calie then raced to wake up all the other shepherds who were sleeping nearby.

As the shepherds awoke they said, "What does this dog want? Why is he waking us?"

Calie ran half way down the hill toward the stable hoping they would follow.

The shepherds then noticed a bright star that appeared to shine over a place not too far from them.

They decided to follow the dog and head toward the star.

As the shepherds began to walk an angel
suddenly appeared in front of them.

She said "Do not be afraid because I have good news."

She announced "This evening the Son of God
was born in Bethlehem and His name is Jesus."

The angel told the shepherds to continue
to follow the dog and he would lead them to
the stable where Jesus was lying in the manger.

The shepherds listened to what the angel said and quickly followed Calie.

When they arrived at the stable they were greeted by Mary and Joseph and proceeded to kneel down in front of the manger.

They were overjoyed and filled with awe at the sight of the baby, Jesus.

The shepherds told Mary and Joseph how an angel appeared to them and told them about the birth of Jesus and that they should follow the dog to the stable.

The shepherds stayed to appreciate the wonder of what they experienced but eventually they needed to return to their sheep.

Calie remained at the stable to be with Jesus, Mary and Joseph.

At the same time the
shepherds arrived at
the stable, there were
three kings in the East
who saw a magnificent
star in the sky.
They had never seen
anything like it before.

They decided to follow the star
and explore what might be taking place.

The kings packed their camels with special gifts of
gold, frankincense and myrrh and set out for what
would be a long journey to Bethlehem.

As the kings approached the town they saw that the star was positioned directly over a stable.

They stopped to consider what this meant and what they should do.

Standing guard outside the stable Calie saw the profile of the kings on the crest of a hill. He immediately got up, stretched and began to run toward them.

When he reached them, he sat and looked up at the camels. He barked and turned to lead them to Jesus.

When the kings arrived at the stable Mary guided them over to the manger.

They were amazed when they saw the baby, Jesus. They immediately knelt down and placed their gifts on the ground in front of the manger.

The kings remained in silent adoration until it was time for them to return home.

Calie stayed at the stable with Mary and Joseph
to keep watch over them and Jesus.

Soon after the kings left, an angel appeared to Joseph and told him to leave Bethlehem and take his family to Egypt.

Joseph packed their belongings and helped Mary onto a donkey with Jesus in her arms. Calie sat close by and watched, without making a sound.

As they departed the dog started to follow them but quickly stopped. With his tail down, he stood sadly in front of the stable until they were out of sight.

With his head bowed, Calie walked slowly away
from the stable and back to where
the sheep were gathered.

To his surprise, he heard Eli's voice calling him
and he started to run. When Calie saw the shepherd
kneeling down in front of him his whole body
wagged and he jumped with joy.

He had shared in a miracle
and now he was home.

Epilogue

# Unconditional Love

The dog was the shepherd's faithful friend.
He was his partner. He loved him unconditionally.
This meant he loved the shepherd
no matter what happened.

He loved him during good times and bad.

Jesus also loves us unconditionally.
He is forgiving. He is always with us.
His love never ends.

# BIOGRAPHY NOTES

## AUTHOR
### Richard J. Kinney

Dick Kinney was raised in New Jersey but now calls South Carolina home. He is a graduate of Fairfield University in Connecticut and is now retired after an extensive, successful business career.

He and his wife, Suzanne, with whom he will celebrate their golden anniversary next year, have four grown sons and, of course, a dog, Connolly, a soft coated wheaten terrier.

## ARTIST
### Sandy Huston

Sandy Huston earned a Bachelors of Art degree from Rowan University and has been working in the field of art for 40 years. Her jobs include: illustration artist, screen printer, muralist, high school art teacher and graphic artist at School Publications Inc.

Sandy continues to pursue a career in fine art by participating in many local and regional art shows. She was accepted in the Pastel Society of America and began showing in galleries in New York City. For the past 15 years, Sandy has owned Monet's Garden Art Studio, located in Ocean Grove, New Jersey where these beautiful illustrations were created.

CPSIA information can be obtained at www.ICGtesting.com
Printed in the USA
BVOW10*2336091215

428520BV00006B/2/P